Small Babies

Jacqueline McQuade

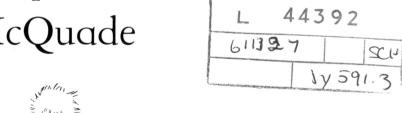

DAVID BENNETT BOOKS

Baby
Mice

A baby mouse does not have a special name.
These tiny baby mice are sharing a juicy piece of apple.

Otter
Cub

A baby otter is called a cub.
This little otter cub stays close to the riverbank
when she goes swimming on her own.

Baby
Bunnies

A baby rabbit should be called a kitten
but the word 'bunny' is more popular.
These baby bunnies are brother and sister
and they love to cuddle up to each other.

Raccoon Cub

A baby raccoon is called a cub.
This raccoon cub loves to spend his time climbing trees.

Baby
Koala

A baby koala does not have a special name.
*This cute little koala clings onto his mummy's back
and just enjoys the ride!*

Owlets

A baby owl is called an owlet.
*These fluffy owlets are waiting for their mummy
to bring them something to eat.*

Baby
Guinea Pigs

A baby guinea pig does not have a special name.
These baby guinea pigs can be quite mischievous –
just look what they have done to these balls of wool!

Baby Squirrels

A baby squirrel does not have a special name.
*These little squirrels are already old enough to climb trees
and they love to play hide-and-seek.*